Hippocrene

CHILDREN'S
ILLUSTRATED
CHINESE
(Mandarin)
DICTIONARY

ENGLISH · CHINESE
CHINESE · ENGLISH

Compiled and translated by the Editors of Hippocrene Books

Interior illustrations by S. Grant (24, 81, 88); J. Gress (page 10, 21, 24, 37, 46, 54, 59, 65, 72, 75, 77);
K. Migliorelli (page 13, 14, 18, 19, 20, 21, 22, 25, 31, 32, 37, 39, 40, 46, 47, 66, 71, 75, 76, 82, 86, 87);
B. Swidzinska (page 9, 11, 12, 13, 14, 16, 23, 27, 28, 30, 32, 33, 35, 37, 38, 41, 42, 45, 46, 47, 48, 49, 50,
52, 53, 56, 57, 58, 59, 60, 61, 62, 63, 66, 68, 69, 70, 71, 72, 73, 75, 77, 78, 79, 83), N. Zhukov (page 8, 13,
14, 17, 18, 23, 27, 29, 33, 34, 39, 40, 41, 52, 64, 65, 71, 72, 73, 78, 84, 86, 88).

Design, prepress, and production: Graafiset International, Inc.

Cataloging-in-Publication Data available from the Library of Congress.

ISBN 0-7818-0848-0

Printed in China

For information, address:
Hippocrene Books, Inc.
171 Madison Avenue
New York, NY 10016
www.hippocrenebooks.com

INTRODUCTION

With their absorbent minds, infinite curiosities and excellent memories, children have enormous capacities to master many languages. All they need is exposure and encouragement.

The easiest way to learn a foreign language is to simulate the same natural method by which a child learns English. The natural technique is built on the concept that language is representational of concrete objects and ideas. The use of pictures and words are the natural way for children to begin to acquire a new language.

The concept of this Illustrated Dictionary is to allow children to build vocabulary and initial competency naturally. Looking at the pictorial content of the Dictionary and saying and matching the words in connection to the drawings gives children the opportunity to discover the foreign language and thus, a new way to communicate.

The drawings in the Dictionary are designed to capture children's imaginations and make the learning process interesting and entertaining, as children return to a word and picture repeatedly until they begin to recognize it.

The beautiful images and clear presentation make this dictionary a wonderful tool for unlocking your child's multilingual potential.

Deborah Dumont, M.A., M.Ed.,
Child Psychologist and Educational Consultant

Chinese Pronunciation

Transliteration	Approximate English equivalent	Transliteration	Approximate English equivalent
a	as in father	uan	as in Taiwan
ao	as in now	uang	as in oo + hung
ai	as in kite		
an	as in man	ui	as in weigh
ang	as in hung	un	as in went
o	as in lore	ü	as in French tu
ou	as in tow	üan	as in ü + an
ong	as in own	üe	as in ü + eh
		ün	as in German grün
e	as in nurse		
ei	as in make	b	as in bat
en	as in turn	p	as in pat
eng	as in sung	m	as in map
er	as in err	f	as in fat
		d	as in dad
i	as in meet	t	as in take
i (after z, c, s, zh, ch, sh and r)	(silent)	n	as in night
		l	as in let
ia	as in yacht	g	as in go
iao	as in meow	k	as in key
ian	as in yen	h	as in hop
iang	as in young	j	as in jump
iong	as in German jünger	q	as in cheese
ie	as in yes	x	as in sheep
iu	as in yoke	z	as in odds
in	as in pin	c	as in hats
ing	as in ping	s	as in sand
		zh	as in rouge
u	as in rude	ch	as in charge
ua	as in watch	sh	as in sharp
uo	as in wall	r	as in ray
uai	as in wait		

Conventions of Romanization (Pinyin)

1. i is written as y when it occurs at the beginning of a syllable, e.g. ie → ey, ian → yan. i is written as yi when it forms a syllable by itself, e.g. i → yi.
2. u is written as w when it occurs at the beginning of a syllable, e.g. uo → wo, uan → wan. u is written as wu when it forms a syllable by itself, e.g. u → wu.
3. ü is written as yu when it occurs at the beginning of a syllable or forms a syllable by itself, e.g. üe → yüe, üan →üan, ü → yu.
4. i does not have any phonetic value when it follows z, c, s, zh, ch, sh and r.
5. When preceded by a consonant, uei and uen become ui and un.
6. ü is written as u after j, q, x and y.

Tones

Chinese is a tone language. Variations of the pitch result in different meanings. In Mandarin Chinese, there are four tones, which are referred to as the first tone, the second tone, the third tone and the fourth tone and are indicated, respectively, by the tone graphs – ˊ ˇ ˋ . The first tone is called highĭlevel tone. As the name suggests, it should be high, almost at the upper limit of the pitch range, and level, without any fluctuation. The second tone is called rising tone. It starts from the middle of the pitch range and rises. The third tone is called fallingĭrising tone. As such, it has two parts: first falling, then rising. It moves down from the lower half of the pitch range and moves up to a point near the top. The fourth tone is called falling tone. It falls precipitously all the way down from the top of the pitch level. In addition to the four tones, Mandarin Chinese has a "fifth" tone, which is actually a toneless tone. As such it is usually called neutral tone. Its pronunciation is soft and quick. The neutral tone is not diacritically marked. It occurs either on grammatical particles or the second syllable of some words that do not receive stress.

airplane　　　飞机
　　　　　　　　fēi-jī

alligator　　　鳄鱼
　　　　　　　　è-yú

alphabet　　　字母表
　　　　　　　　zì-mǔ-biǎo

antelope　　　羚羊
　　　　　　　　líng-yáng

antlers　　　鹿角
　　　　　　　　lù-jiǎo

apple 苹果
píng-guǒ

aquarium 养鱼缸
yǎng-yú-gāng

arch 拱形门
gòng-xíng-mén

arrow 箭
jiàn

autumn 秋天
qiū-tiān

baby　　　婴孩
　　　　　　yīng-hái

backpack　　背包
　　　　　　　bēi-bāo

badger　　穴熊
　　　　　　xué-xióng

baker　　面包师
　　　　　miàn-bāo-shī

ball　　　球
　　　　　　qiú

balloon　　气球
　　　　　　qì-qiú

banana
香蕉
xiāng-jiāo

barley
大麦
dà-mài

barrel
桶
tǒng

basket
篮子
lán-zi

bat
蝙蝠
biǎn-fú

beach
海滩
hǎi-tān

bear   熊
xióng

beaver   海狸
hǎi-lí

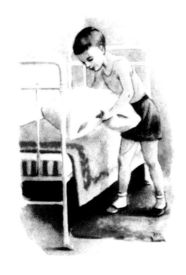

bed   床
chuáng

bee   蜜蜂
mì-fēng

beetle   甲壳虫
jiá-kè-chóng

bell   铃
líng

belt　　皮带
pí-dài

bench　　长椅
cháng-yǐ

bicycle　　自行车
zì-xíng-chē

binoculars　　望远镜
wàng-yuǎn-jìng

bird　　鸟
niǎo

birdcage　　鸟笼
niǎo-lóng

black　　　黑色
　　　　　　hēi-sè

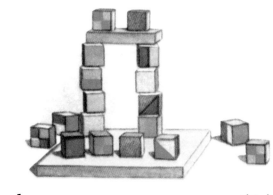

blocks　　　积木
　　　　　　jī-mù

blossom　　　开花
　　　　　　kāi-huā

blue　　　蓝色
　　　　　lán-sè

boat　　　船
　　　　　chuán

bone　　　骨头
　　　　　gú-tou

book 书
shū

boot 靴子
xuē-zi

bottle 瓶子
píng-zi

bowl 碗
wǎn

boy 男孩
nán-hái

bracelet 手镯
shǒu-zhuó

branch 树枝
shù-zhī

bread 面包
miàn-bāo

breakfast 早饭
zǎo-fàn

bridge 桥
qiáo

broom 笤帚
tiáo-zhǒu

brother 兄弟
xiōng-dì

brown

棕色
zōng-sè

brush

刷子
shuā-zi

bucket

水桶
shuǐ-tǒng

bulletin board

布告栏
bù-gào-lán

bumblebee

黄蜂
huáng-fēng

butterfly

蝴蝶
hú-dié

cab   出租车
chū-zū-chē

cabbage   大白菜
dà-bái-cài

cactus   仙人掌
xiān-rén-zhǎng

café   咖啡馆
kā-fēi-guǎn

cake   蛋糕
dàn-gāo

camel   骆驼
luò-tuo

camera 照相机
zhào-xiàng-jī

candle 蜡烛
là-zhú

candy 糖果
táng-guǒ

canoe 独木舟
dú-mù-zhōu

cap 帽子
mào-zi

captain 船长
chuán-zhǎng

car

汽车
qì-chē

card

扑克牌
pū-kè-pái

carpet

地毯
dì-tǎn

carrot

胡萝卜
hú-luó-bo

(to) carry

拎
līng

castle

城堡
chéng-bǎo

cat

猫
māo

cave

山洞
shān-dòng

chair

椅子
yǐ-zi

cheese

奶酪
nǎi-lào

cherry

樱桃
yīng-táo

chimney

烟囱
yān-cong

chocolate

巧克力
qiǎo-kè-lì

Christmas tree

圣诞树
shèng-dàn-shù

circus

马戏团
mǎ-xì-tuán

(to) climb

爬
pá

cloud

云
yún

clown

小丑
xiǎo-chǒu

coach　　　马车
mǎ-chē

coat　　　大衣
dà-yī

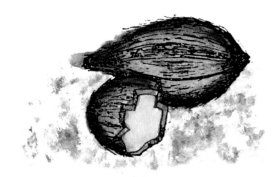

coconut　　　椰子
yē-zi

comb　　　梳子
shū-zi

comforter　　　被子
bèi-zi

compass　　　指南针
zhǐ-nán-zhēn

(to) cook 做饭
zuò-fàn

cork 木塞
mù-sāi

corn 玉米
yù-mǐ

cow 母牛
mǔ-niú

cracker 饼干
bǐng-gān

cradle 摇篮
yáo-lán

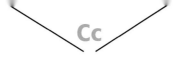

(to) crawl 爬
pá

(to) cross 过马路
guò-mǎ-lù

crown 皇冠
huáng-guān

(to) cry 哭
kū

cucumber 黄瓜
huáng-guā

curtain 窗帘
chuāng-lián

(to) dance

跳舞
tiào-wǔ

dandelion

蒲公英
pǔ-gōng-yīng

date

日期
rì-qī

deer

鹿
lù

desert

沙漠
shā-mò

desk

书桌
shū-zhuō

dirty

脏
zāng

dog

狗
gǒu

doghouse

狗屋
gǒu-wū

doll

洋娃娃
yáng-wá-wa

dollhouse

洋娃娃屋
yáng-wá-wa-wū

dolphin

海豚
hǎi-tún

donkey

驴子
lǘ-zi

dragon

龙
lóng

dragonfly 蜻蜓
qīng-tíng

(to) draw 画画
huà-huà

dress 连衣裙
lián-yī-qún

(to) drink 喝
hē

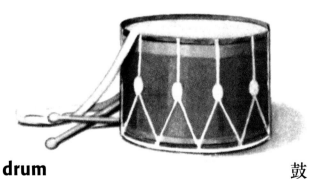

drum 鼓
gǔ

duck 鸭子
yā-zi

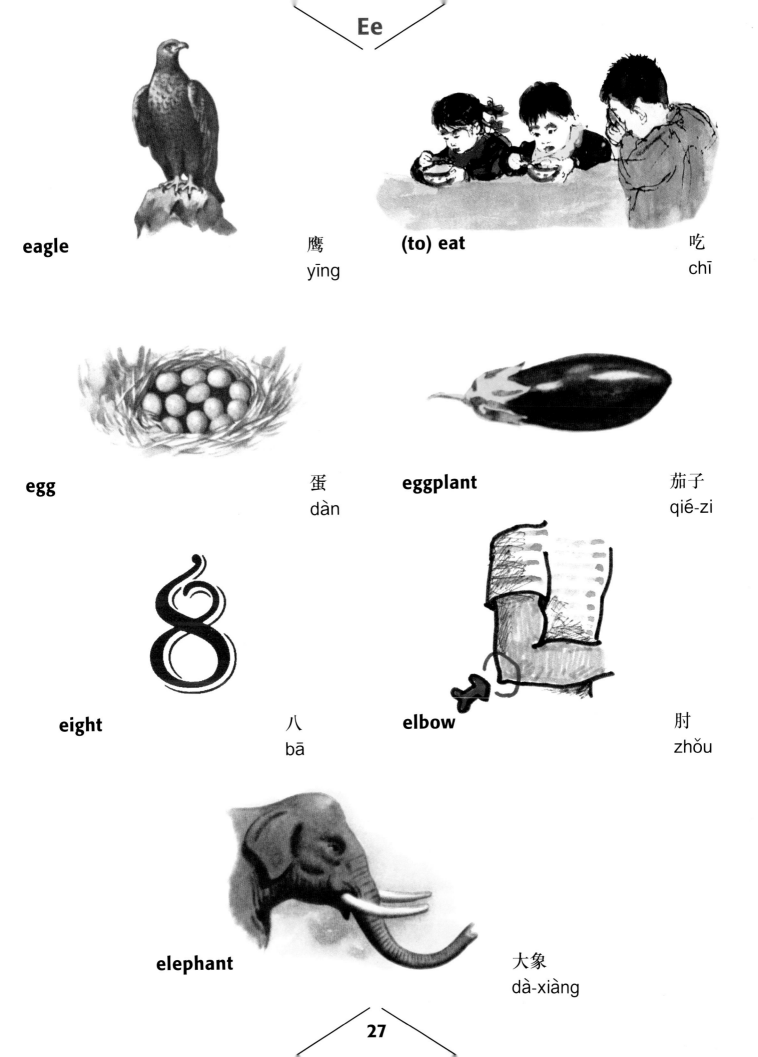

eagle 鹰
yīng

(to) eat 吃
chī

egg 蛋
dàn

eggplant 茄子
qié-zi

eight 八
bā

elbow 肘
zhǒu

elephant 大象
dà-xiàng

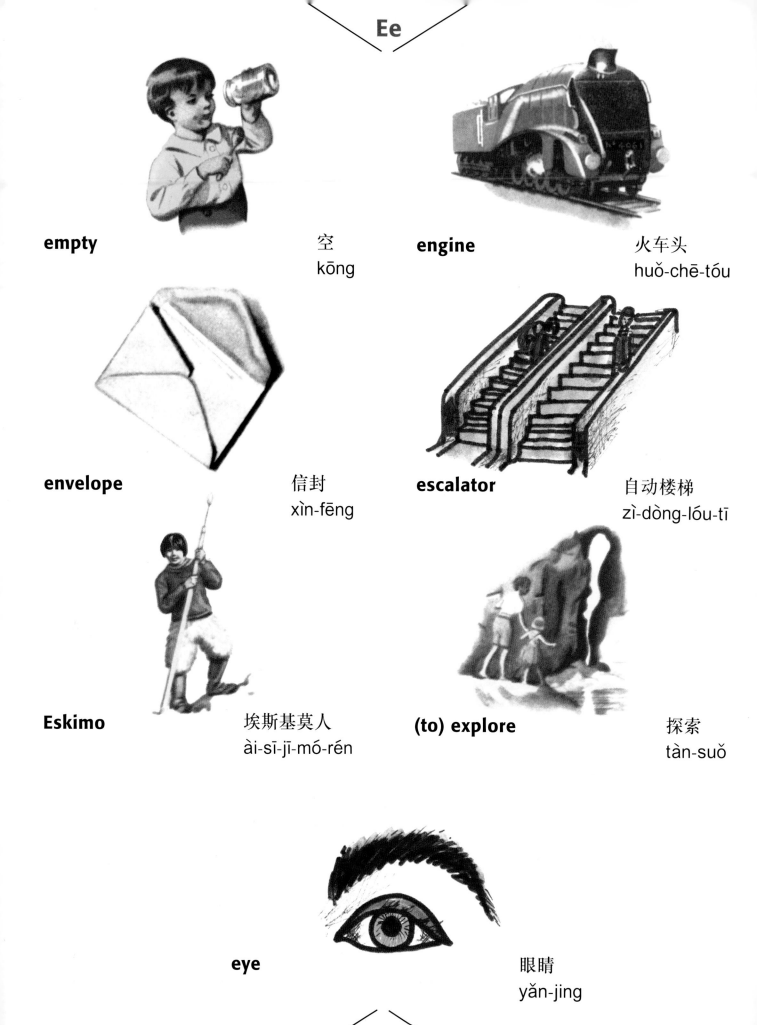

empty　　　　　　空
　　　　　　　　　kōng

engine　　　　　火车头
　　　　　　　　　huǒ-chē-tóu

envelope　　　　信封
　　　　　　　　　xìn-fēng

escalator　　　　自动楼梯
　　　　　　　　　zì-dòng-lóu-tī

Eskimo　　　　　埃斯基莫人
　　　　　　　　　ài-sī-jī-mó-rén

(to) explore　　探索
　　　　　　　　　tàn-suǒ

eye　　　　　　眼睛
　　　　　　　　　yǎn-jing

face 脸
liǎn

fan 电扇
diàn-shàn

father 爸爸
bà-ba

fear 害怕
hài-pà

feather 羽毛
yǔ-máo

(to) feed 喂
wèi

fence 栅栏
zhà-lan

fern 蕨
jué

field 田
tián

field mouse 田鼠
tián-shǔ

finger 手指
shǒu-zhǐ

fir tree 枞树
cōng-shù

fire   火
          huǒ

fish   鱼
                              yú

(to) fish   钓鱼
                              diào-yú

fist   拳头
                              quán-tou

five   五
                              wǔ

flag   旗
                              qí

Ff

flashlight 电筒 diàn-tǒng

(to) float 飘 piāo

flower 花 huā

(to) fly 飞 fēi

foot 脚 jiǎo

fork 叉 chā

fountain 喷泉 pēng-quán

four 四
sì

fox 狐狸
hú-li

frame 镜框
jìng-kuāng

friend 朋友
péng-you

frog 青蛙
qīng-wā

fruit 水果
shuǐ-guǒ

furniture 家具
jiā-jù

garden 花园
huā-yuán

gate 大门
dà-mén

(to) gather 采
cǎi

geranium 天竺葵
tiān-zhú-kuí

giraffe 长颈鹿
cháng-jǐng-lù

girl 女孩
nǚ-hái

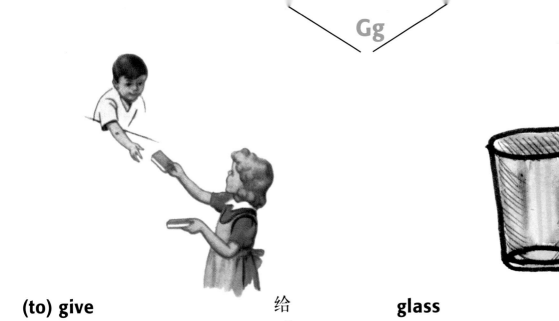

(to) give　　给
　　　　　　　gěi

glass　　玻璃
　　　　　　bō-lí

glasses　　眼镜
　　　　　　　yǎn-jìng

globe　　地球仪
　　　　　　dì-qiú-yí

glove　　手套
　　　　　　shǒu-tào

goat　　山羊
　　　　　shān-yáng

goldfish   金鱼
jīn-yú

"Good Night"   晚安
wǎn-ān

"Good-bye"   再见
zài-jiàn

goose   鹅
é

grandfather   爷爷，外公
yé-ye (paternal),
wài-gōng (maternal)

grandmother   奶奶，外婆
nǎi-nai (paternal),
wài-pó (maternal)

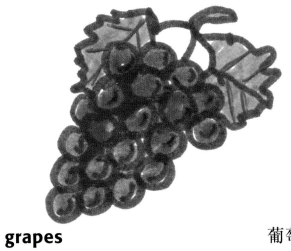

grapes　　　　葡萄
pú-tao

grasshopper　　蚂蚱
mà-zha

green　　　　绿色
lǜ-sè

greenhouse　　温室
wēn-shì

guitar　　　　吉它
jí-tā

hammer 锤子
chuí-zi

hammock 吊床
diào-chuáng

hamster 仓鼠
cāng-shǔ

hand 手
shǒu

handbag 手提包
shǒu-tí-bāo

handkerchief 手绢
shǒu-juàn

harvest　收获
shōu-huò

hat　帽子
mào-zi

hay　干草
gān-cǎo

headdress　头饰
tóu-shì

heart　心
xīn

hedgehog　豪猪
háo-zhū

hen 母鸡
mǔ-jī

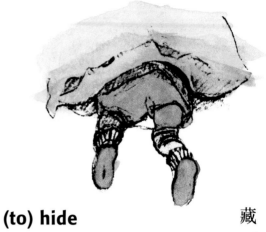

(to) hide 藏
cáng

highway 公路
gōng-lù

honey 蜂蜜
fēng-mì

horns 角
jiǎo

horse 马
mǎ

horseshoe

马掌
mǎ-zhǎng

hourglass

沙漏
shā-lòu

house

房子
fáng-zi

(to) hug

拥抱
yōng-bào

hydrant

消防栓
xiāo-fáng-shuān

ice cream　　冰淇淋
bīng-qí-lín

ice cubes　　冰块
bīng-kuà

ice-skating　　溜冰
liū-bīng

instrument　　乐器
yuè-qì

iris　　蝴蝶花
hú-dié-huā

iron　　熨斗
yùn-dǒu

island　　岛
dǎo

jacket　　　　上衣
　　　　　　　　shàng-yī

jam　　　　酱
　　　　　　jiàng

jigsaw puzzle　　拼板玩具
　　　　　　　　　pīn-bǎn-wán-jù

jockey　　　赛马骑师
　　　　　　　sài-mǎ-qí-shī

juggler　　　杂耍师
　　　　　　　zá-shuǎ-shī

(to) jump　　　跳
　　　　　　　　tiào

kangaroo　　　袋鼠
dài-shǔ

key　　　钥匙
yào-shi

kitten　　　小猫
xiǎo-māo

knife　　　刀
dāo

knight　　　骑士
qí-shì

(to) knit　　　织
zhī

knot　　　结
jié

koala bear　　　无尾熊
wú-wěi-xióng

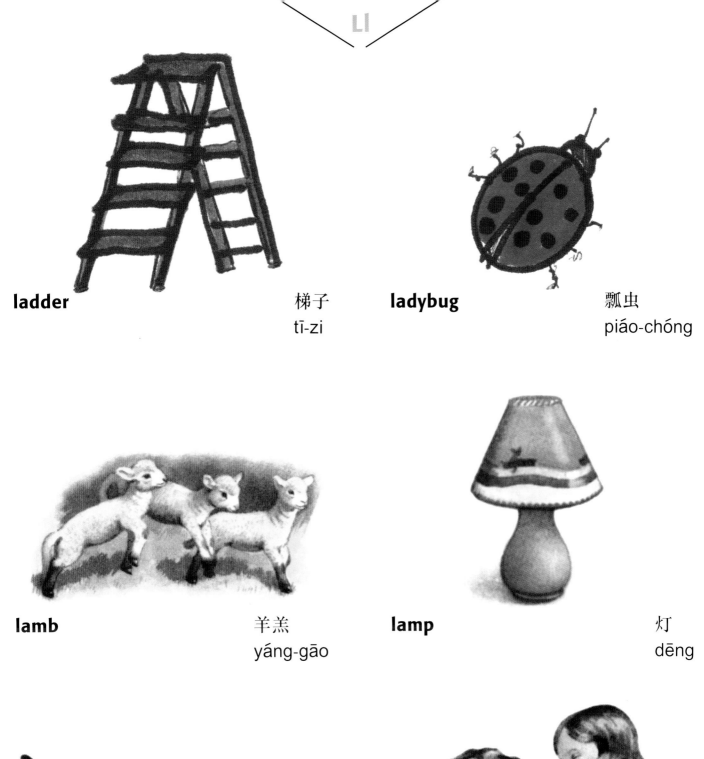

ladder 梯子
tī-zi

ladybug 瓢虫
piáo-chóng

lamb 羊羔
yáng-gāo

lamp 灯
dēng

(to) lap 舔
tiǎn

laughter 笑
xiào

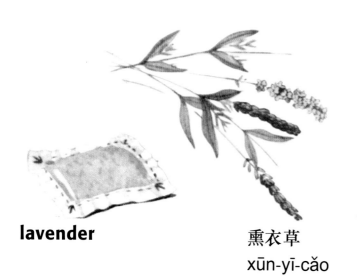

lavender

熏衣草
xūn-yī-cǎo

lawn mower

除草机
chú-cǎo-jī

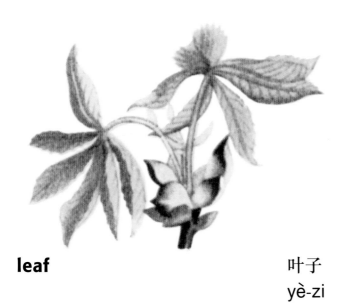

leaf

叶子
yè-zi

leg

腿
tuǐ

lemon

柠檬
níng-méng

lettuce

生菜
shēng-cài

lightbulb 灯泡
dēng-pào

lighthouse 灯塔
dēng-tǎ

lilac 丁香花
dīng-xiāng-huā

lion 狮子
shī-zi

(to) listen 听
tīng

lobster 龙虾
lóng-xiā

lock 锁
suǒ

lovebird 相思鸟
xiāng-sī-niǎo

luggage 行李
xíng-li

lumberjack 伐木工人
fá-mù-gōng-rén

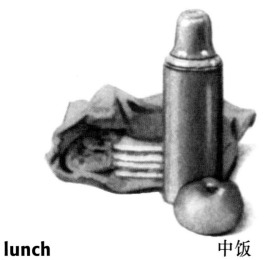

lunch 中饭
zhōng-fàn

lynx 山猫
shān-māo

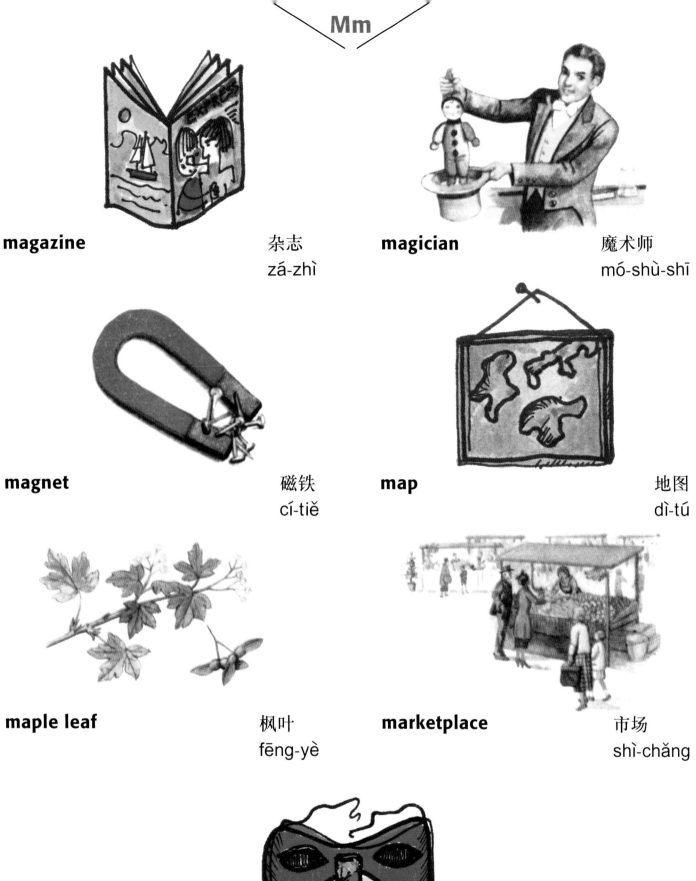

magazine　　杂志
　　　　　　　zá-zhì

magician　　魔术师
　　　　　　　mó-shù-shī

magnet　　　磁铁
　　　　　　　cí-tiě

map　　　　　地图
　　　　　　　dì-tú

maple leaf　枫叶
　　　　　　　fēng-yè

marketplace　市场
　　　　　　　shì-chǎng

mask　　　　　面具
　　　　　　　miàn-jù

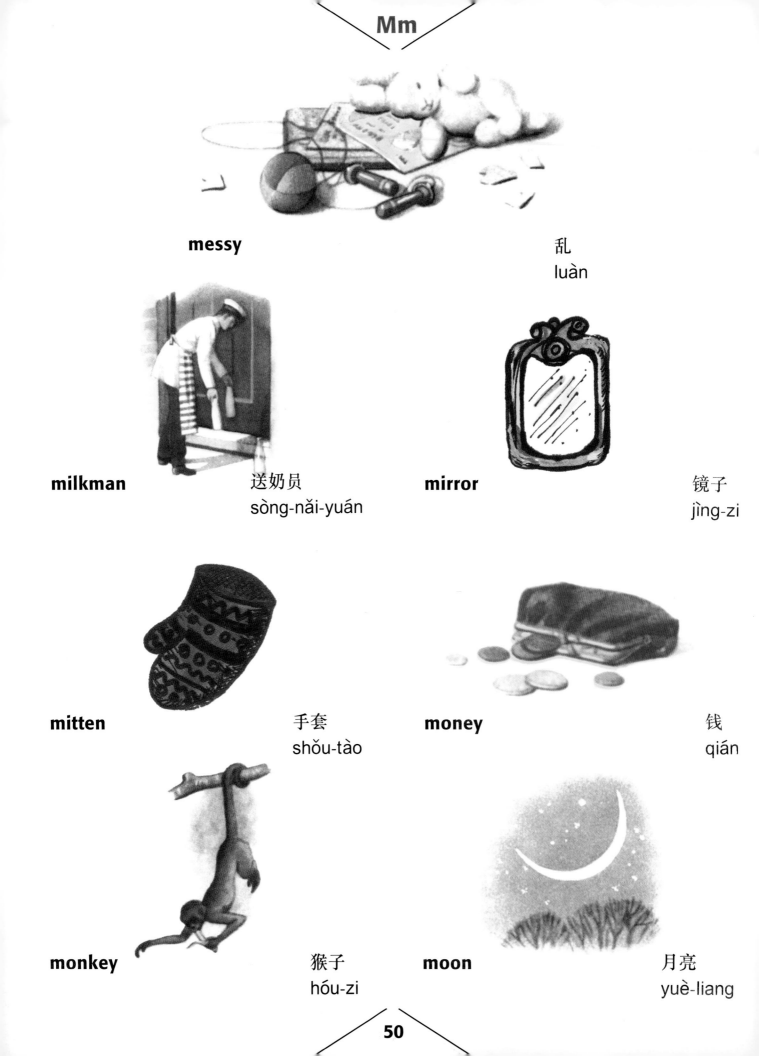

messy

乱
luàn

milkman

送奶员
sòng-nǎi-yuán

mirror

镜子
jìng-zi

mitten

手套
shǒu-tào

money

钱
qián

monkey

猴子
hóu-zi

moon

月亮
yuè-liang

Mm

mother　　　妈妈
　　　　　　　mā-ma

mountain　　　山
　　　　　　　　shān

mouse　　　老鼠
　　　　　　lǎo-shǔ

mouth　　　嘴
　　　　　　zuǐ

mushroom　　　蘑菇
　　　　　　　mó-gū

music　　　音乐
　　　　　yīn-yuè

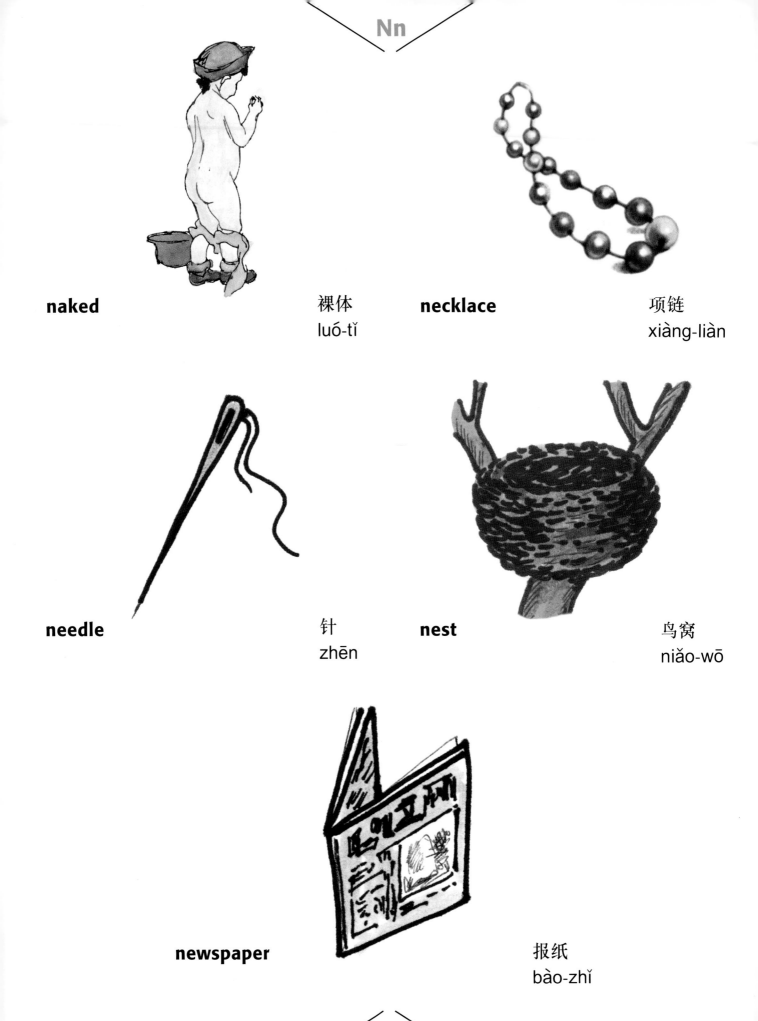

naked　　　　裸体
　　　　　　　luó-tǐ

necklace　　　项链
　　　　　　　xiàng-liàn

needle　　　针
　　　　　　　zhēn

nest　　　鸟窝
　　　　　　　niǎo-wō

newspaper　　　报纸
　　　　　　　bào-zhǐ

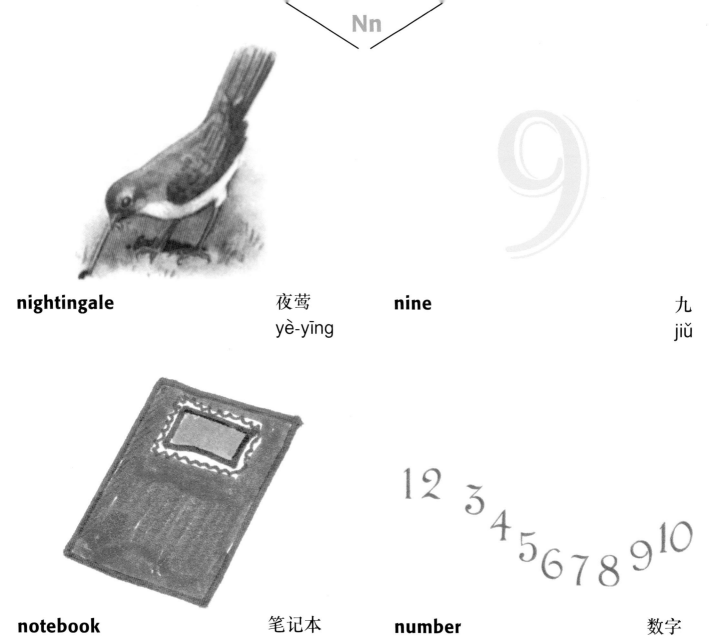

nightingale 夜莺
yè-yīng

nine 九
jiǔ

notebook 笔记本
bǐ-jì-běn

number 数字
shù-zi

nut 果子
guǒ-zi

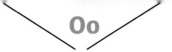

oar   桨
                           jiǎng

ocean liner   远洋客轮
                   yuǎn-yáng-kè-lún

old   老
               lǎo

one   一
               yī

onion   洋葱
                 yáng-cōng

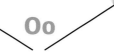

open 开
kāi

orange 橘子
jú-zi

ostrich 鸵鸟
tuó-niǎo

owl 猫头鹰
māo-tóu-yīng

ox 公牛
gōng-niú

padlock
挂锁
guà-suǒ

paint
颜料
yán-liào

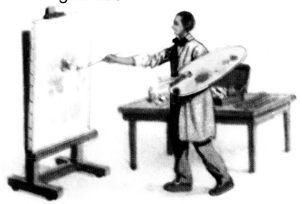

painter
画家
huà-jiā

pajamas
睡衣
shuì-yī

palm tree
棕榈
zōng-lǘ

paper
纸
zhǐ

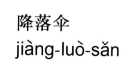

parachute
降落伞
jiàng-luò-sǎn

park

公园
gōng-yuán

parrot

鹦鹉
yīng-wū

passport

护照
hù-zhào

patch

补丁
bǔ-ding

path

小径
xiǎo-jìng

peach

桃子
táo-zi

pear

梨子
lí-zi

pebble

鹅卵石
é-luǎn-shí

(to) peck

啄
zhuó

(to) peel

剥皮
bó-pí

pelican

鹈鹕
tí-hú

pencil

铅笔
qiān-bǐ

penguin

企鹅
qǐ-é

people

人
rén

piano
钢琴
gāng-qín

pickle
泡黄瓜
pào-huáng-guā

pie
馅饼
xiàn-bǐng

pig
猪
zhū

pigeon
鸽子
gē-zi

pillow
枕头
zhěn-tou

pin
大头针
dà-tóu-zhēn

pine

松树
sōng-shù

pineapple

菠萝
bō-luó

pit

果核
guǒ-hé

pitcher

水罐
shuǐ-guàn

plate

盘子
pán-zi

platypus

鸭嘴兽
yā-zuǐ-shòu

(to) play 玩
wán

plum 李子
lǐ-zi

polar bear 北极熊
běi-jí-xióng

pony 小马
xiǎo-mǎ

pot 锅
guō

potato 土豆
tǔ-dòu

(to) pour　　　　倒
dào

present　　　　礼物
lǐ-wù

(to) pull　　　　拉
lā

pumpkin　　　　南瓜
nán-guā

Qq

puppy　　　　小狗
xiǎo-gǒu

queen　　　　女皇
nǚ-huáng

rabbit

兔子
tù-zi

raccoon

浣熊
huàn-xióng

racket

球拍
qiú-pāi

radio

收音机
shōu-yīn-jī

radish

萝卜
luó-bo

raft 橡皮船
xiàng-pí-chuán

rain 雨
yǔ

rainbow 彩虹
cǎi-hóng

raincoat 雨衣
yǔ-yī

raspberry 木莓
mù-méi

(to) read

读书
dú-shū

red

红色
hóng-sè

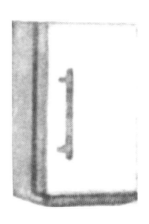

refrigerator

冰箱
bīng-xiāng

rhinoceros

犀牛
xī-niú

ring

戒指
jiè-zhī

(to) ring 打铃
dǎ-líng

river 河
hé

road 路
lù

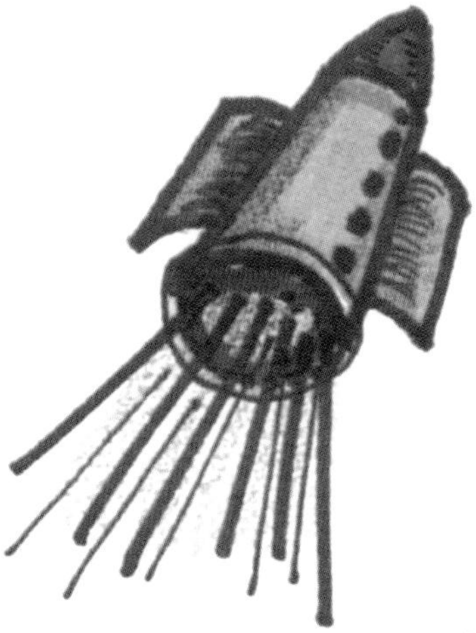

rocket 火箭
huǒ-jiàn

roof 房顶
fáng-dǐng

rooster 公鸡
gōng-jī

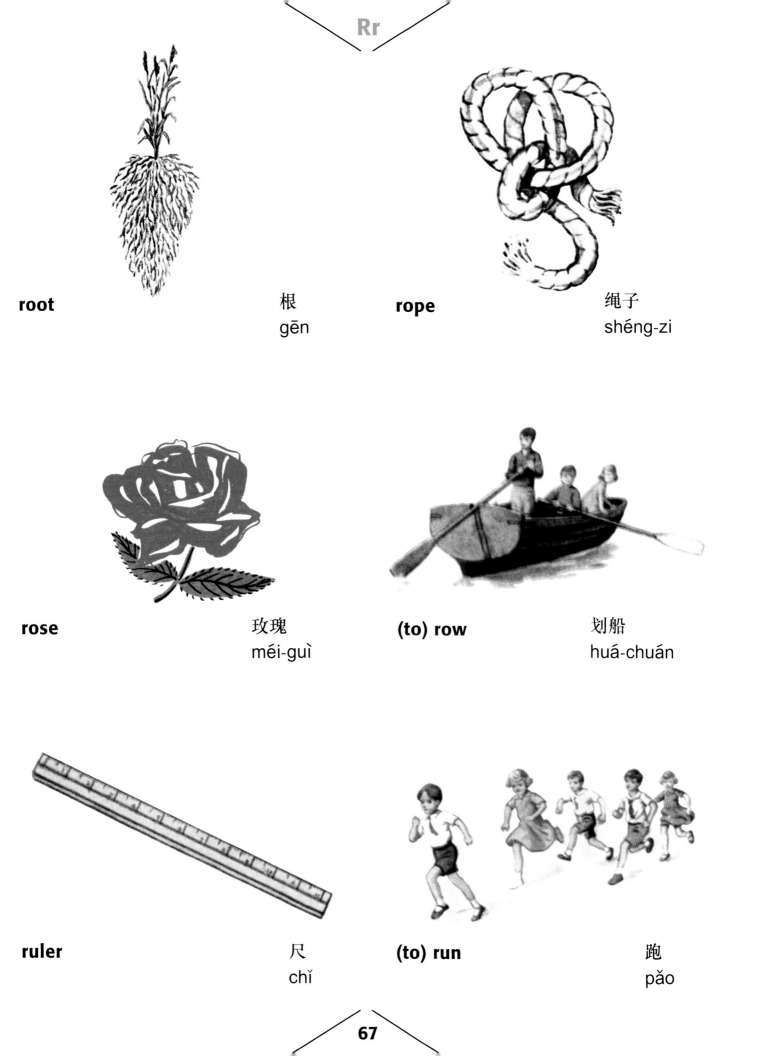

root 根
gēn

rope 绳子
shéng-zi

rose 玫瑰
méi-guì

(to) row 划船
huá-chuán

ruler 尺
chǐ

(to) run 跑
pǎo

safety pin
别针
bié-zhēn

(to) sail
扬帆航行
yáng-fān-háng-xíng

sailor
水手
shuǐ-shǒu

salt
盐
yán

scarf
围巾
wéi-jīn

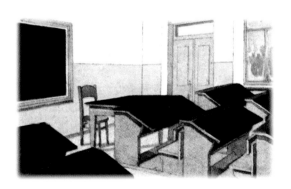

school
学校
xué-xiào

scissors　　　　剪刀
　　　　　　　　jiǎn-dāo

screwdriver　　　螺丝刀
　　　　　　　　luó-sī-dāo

seagull　　　　海鸥
　　　　　　　hǎi-ōu

seesaw　　　　跷跷板
　　　　　　　qiào-qiào-bǎn

seven　　　　七
　　　　　　qī

(to) sew　　　缝
　　　　　　　féng

shark
鲨鱼
shā-yú

sheep
绵羊
mián-yáng

shell
贝壳
bèi-ké

shepherd
牧羊人
mù-yáng-rén

ship
船
chuán

shirt
衬衫
chèn-shān

shoe 鞋子
xié-zi

shovel 铁锹
tiě-xiān

(to) show 给看
gěi-kàn

shower 淋浴
lín-yù

shutter 百叶窗
bǎi-yè-chuāng

sick 生病
shēng-bìng

sieve　　　筛子
shāi-zi

(to) sing　　　唱歌
chàng-gē

(to) sit　　　坐
zuò

six　　　六
liù

sled　　　雪橇
xuě-qiāo

(to) sleep　　　睡觉
shuì-jiào

small 小
xiǎo

smile 笑
xiào

snail 蜗牛
wō-niú

snake 蛇
shé

snow 雪
xuě

sock 袜子
wà-zi

sofa 沙发
shā-fā

sparrow 麻雀
má-què

spider 蜘蛛
zhī-zhū

spiderweb 蜘蛛网
zhī-zhū-wǎng

spoon 汤匙
tāng-chí

squirrel 松鼠
sōng-shǔ

stairs 楼梯
lóu-tī

stamp 邮票
yóu-piào

starfish 海星
hǎi-xīng

stork 白鹳
bái-guàn

stove 煤气炉
méi-qì-lú

strawberry 草莓
cǎo-méi

subway　　　　地铁
dì-tiě

sugar cube　　糖块
táng-kuài

sun　　　　太阳
tài-yáng

sunflower　　向日葵
xiàng-rì-kuí

sweater　　毛衣
máo-yī

(to) sweep　　扫地
sǎo-dì

swing　　荡秋千
dàng-qiū-qiān

table 桌子
zhuō-zi

teapot 茶壶
chá-hú

teddy bear 玩具熊
wán-jù-xióng

television 电视
diàn-shì

10

ten 十
shí

tent 帐篷
zhàng-peng

theater 剧院
jù-yuàn

thimble 顶针
dǐng-zhēn

(to) think 想
xiǎng

3

three 三
sān

tie 领带
lǐng-dài

(to) tie 系
jì

tiger 老虎
lǎo-hǔ

toaster 烤面包片器
kǎo-miàn-bāo-piàn-qì

tomato 番茄
fān-qié

toucan 巨嘴鸟
jù-zuǐ-niǎo

towel 毛巾
máo-jīn

tower 塔
tǎ

toy box 玩具箱
wán-jù-xiāng

tracks 铁轨
tiě-guǐ

train station 火车站
huǒ-chē-zhàn

tray 端盘
duān-pán

tree 树
shù

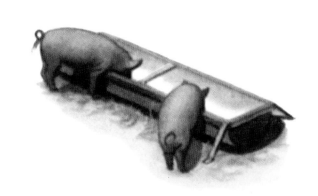

trough 猪槽
zhū-cáo

truck

卡车
kǎ-chē

trumpet

小号
xiǎo-hào

tulip

郁金香
yù-jīn-xiāng

tunnel

隧道
suì-dào

turtle

乌龟
wū-guī

twins

双胞胎
shuāng-bāo-tāi

two

二
èr

umbrella   伞
sǎn

uphill   上坡
shàng-pō

Vv

vase   花瓶
huā-píng

veil   面纱
miàn-shā

V v

village

村庄
cūn-zhuāng

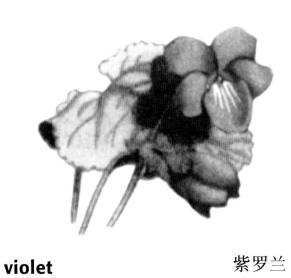

violet

紫罗兰
zǐ-luó-lán

violin

小提琴
xiǎo-tí-qín

voyage

航行
háng-xíng

waiter 侍者
shì-zhě

(to) wake up 醒来
xǐng-lái

walrus 海象
hǎi-xiàng

(to) wash 洗
xǐ

watch 表
biǎo

(to) watch 看
kàn

(to) water
浇水
jiāo-shuǐ

waterfall
瀑布
pù-bù

watering can
浇花壶
jiāo-huā-hú

watermelon
西瓜
xī-guā

weather vane
风信鸡
fēng-xìn-jī

(to) weigh
称
chēng

whale　　鲸鱼
jīng-yú

wheel　　轮子
lún-zi

wheelbarrow　　独轮车
dú-lún-chē

whiskers　　胡须
hú-xū

(to) whisper　　耳语
ěr-yǔ

whistle　　哨子
shào-zi

white 白色
bái-sè

wig 假发
jiǎ-fà

wind 风
fēng

window 窗子
chuāng-zi

wings 翅膀
chì-bǎng

winter 冬天
dōng-tiān

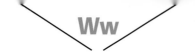

wolf

狼
láng

wood

木头
mù-tou

word

词
cí

(to) write

写
xiě

yellow

黄色
huáng-sè

zebra

斑马
bān-mǎ

Index

A

B

C

D

E

F

Index

féng	(to) sew
fēng	wind
fēng-mì	honey
fēng-xìn-jī	weather vane
fēng-yè	maple leaf

G

gān-cǎo	hay
gāng-qín	piano
gē-zi	pigeon
gěi	(to) give
gěi-kàn	(to) show
gēn	root
gōng-jī	rooster
gōng-lù	highway
gōng-niú	ox
gǒng-xíng-mén	arch
gōng-yuán	park
gǒu	dog
gǒu-wū	doghouse
gǔ	drum
gú-tou	bone
guà-suǒ	padlock
guō	pot
guǒ-hé	pit
guò-mǎ-lù	(to) cross
guǒ-zi	nut

H

hǎi-lí	beaver
hǎi-ōu	seagull
hài-pà	fear
hǎi-tún	dolphin
hǎi-tān	beach

hǎi-xiàng	walrus
hǎi-xīng	starfish
háng-xíng	voyage
háo-zhū	hedgehog
hē	(to) drink
hé	river
hēi-sè	black
hóng-sè	red
hóu-zi	monkey
hú-dié	butterfly
hú-dié-huā	iris
hú-li	fox
hú-luó-bo	carrot
hú-xū	whiskers
hù-zhào	passport
huā	flower
huá-chuán	(to) row
huà-huà	(to) draw
huà-jiā	painter
huā-píng	vase
huā-yuán	garden
huàn-xióng	raccoon
huáng-fēng	bumblebee
huáng-guā	cucumber
huáng-guān	crown
huáng-sè	yellow
huǒ	fire
huǒ-chē-tóu	engine
huǒ-chē-zhàn	train station
huǒ-jiàn	rocket

J

jì	(to) tie
jī-mù	blocks
jí-tā	guitar

jiǎ-fà	wig
jiā-jù	furniture
jiá-kè-chóng	beetle
jiàn	arrow
jiǎn-dāo	scissors
jiàng	jam
jiǎng	oar
jiàng-luò-sǎn	parachute
jiǎo	foot
jiǎo	horns
jiāo-huā-hú	watering can
jiāo-shuǐ	(to) water
jié	knot
jiè-zhī	ring
jīn-yú	goldfish
jìng-kuāng	frame
jīng-yú	whale
jìng-zi	mirror
jiǔ	nine
jù-yuàn	theater
jú-zi	orange
jù-zuǐ-niǎo	toucan
jué	fern

K

kǎ-chē	truck
kā-fēi-guǎn	café
kāi	open
kāi-huā	blossom
kàn	(to) watch
kǎo-miàn-bāo -piàn-qì	toaster
kōng	empty
kū	(to) cry

L

lā	(to) pull
là-zhú	candle
lán-sè	blue
lán-zi	basket
láng	wolf
lǎo	old
lǎo-hǔ	tiger
lǎo-shǔ	mouse
lǐ-wù	present
lí-zi	pear
lí-zi	plum
liǎn	face
lián-yī-qún	dress
lín-yù	shower
líng	bell
līng	(to) carry
líng-dài	tie
líng-yáng	antelope
liù	six
liū-bīng	ice-skating
lóng	dragon
lóng-xiā	lobster
lóu-tī	stairs
lù	deer
lù	road
lù-jiǎo	antlers
lǜ-sè	green
lǘ-zi	donkey
luàn	messy
lún-zi	wheel
luó-bo	radish
luó-sī-dāo	screwdriver
luǒ-tǐ	naked
luò-tuo	camel

M

mǎ	horse
mǎ-chē	coach
mā-ma	mother
má-què	sparrow
mǎ-xì-tuán	circus
mà-zha	grasshopper
mǎ-zhǎng	horseshoe
māo	cat
máo-jīn	towel
māo-tóu-yīng	owl
máo-yī	sweater
mào-zi	cap
mào-zi	hat
méi-guì	rose
méi-qì-lú	stove
mì-fēng	bee
miàn-bāo	bread
miàn-bāo-shī	baker
miàn-jù	mask
miàn-shā	veil
mián-yáng	sheep
mó-gū	mushroom
mó-shù-shī	magician
mǔ-jī	hen
mù-méi	raspberry
mù-sāi	cork
mù-tou	wood
mù-yáng-rén	shepherd

N

nǎi-lào	cheese
nǎi-nai (paternal), wài-pó (maternal)	grandmother
nán-guā	pumpkin
nán-hái	boy
niǎo	bird
niǎo-lóng	birdcage
niǎo-wō	nest
níng-méng	lemon
niú	cow
nǚ-hái	girl
nǚ-huáng	queen

P

pá	(to) climb
pá	(to) crawl
pán-zi	plate
pǎo	(to) run
pào-huáng-guā	pickle
pēng-quán	fountain
péng-you	friend
pí-dài	belt
piāo	(to) float
piáo-chóng	ladybug
pīn-bǎn-wán-jù	jigsaw puzzle
píng-guǒ	apple
píng-zi	bottle
pù-bù	waterfall
pǔ-gōng-yīng	dandelion
pū-kè-pái	card
pú-tao	grapes

Q

qí	flag
qī	seven
qì-chē	car

Index

qǐ-é	penguin
qì-qiú	balloon
qí-shì	knight
qián	money
qiān-bǐ	pencil
qiáo	bridge
qiǎo-kè-lì	chocolate
qiào-qiào-bǎn	seesaw
qié-zi	eggplant
qīng-tíng	dragonfly
qīng-wā	frog
qiú	ball
qiú-pāi	racket
qiū-tiān	autumn
quán-tou	fist

R

rén	people
rì-qī	date

S

sān	three
sǎn	umbrella
sài-mǎ-qí-shī	jockey
sǎo-dì	(to) sweep
shā-fā	sofa
shā-lòu	hourglass
shā-mò	desert
shā-yú	shark
shāi-zi	sieve
shān	mountain
shān-dòng	cave
shān-māo	lynx
shān-yáng	goat
shàng-pō	uphill
shàng-yī	jacket
shào-zi	whistle
shé	snake
shēng-bìng	sick

shēng-cài	lettuce
shèng-dàn-shù	Christmas tree
shéng-zi	rope
shí	ten
shì-chǎng	marketplace
shì-zhě	waiter
shī-zi	lion
shǒu	hand
shōu-huò	harvest
shǒu-juàn	handkerchief
shǒu-tào	glove
shǒu-tào	mitten
shǒu-tí-bāo	handbag
shōu-yīn-jī	radio
shǒu-zhǐ	finger
shǒu-zhuó	bracelet
shū	book
shù	tree
shù-zhī	branch
shū-zhuō	desk
shū-zi	comb
shù-zi	number
shuā-zi	brush
shuāng-bāo-tāi	twins
shuǐ-guàn	pitcher
shuǐ-guǒ	fruit
shuì-jiào	(to) sleep
shuǐ-shǒu	sailor
shuǐ-tǒng	bucket
shuì-yī	pajamas
sì	four
sòng-nǎi-yuán	milkman
sōng-shù	pine

sōng-shǔ	squirrel
suì-dào	tunnel
suǒ	lock

T

tǎ	tower
tài-yáng	sun
tàn-suǒ	(to) explore
tāng-chí	spoon
táng-guǒ	candy
táng-kuài	sugar cube
táo-zi	peach
tí-hú	pelican
tī-zi	ladder
tián	field
tiǎn	(to) lap
tián-shǔ	field mouse
tiān-zhú-kuí	geranium
tiào	(to) jump
tiào-wǔ	(to) dance
tiáo-zhǒu	broom
tiě-guǐ	tracks
tiě-xiān	shovel
tīng	(to) listen
tǒng	barrel
tóu-shì	headdress
tǔ-dòu	potato
tù-zi	rabbit
tuǐ	leg
tuó-niǎo	ostrich

W

wà-zi	sock
wǎn	bowl
wán	(to) play
wǎn-ān	"Good Night"
wán-jù-xiāng	toy box

93

Hippocrene Children's Illustrated Foreign Language Dictionaries

Available in 16 languages!

Hippocrene Children's Illustrated Arabic Dictionary
English-Arabic/Arabic-English
94 pages • 8 1/2 x 11 • $11.95pb • 0-7818-0891-X • (212)

Hippocrene Children's Illustrated Chinese Dictionary
English-Chinese/Chinese-English (Mandarin)
94 pages • 8 1/2 x 11 • $11.95pb • 0-7818-0848-0 • (662)

Hippocrene Children's Illustrated Croatian Dictionary
English-Croatian/Croatian-English
94 pages • 8 1/2 x 11 • $11.95pb • 0-7818-1076-0 • (144)

Hippocrene Children's Illustrated Czech Dictionary
English-Czech/Czech-English
94 pages • 8 1/2 x 11 • $11.95pb • 0-7818-0987-8 • (579)

Hippocrene Children's Illustrated Dutch Dictionary
English-Dutch/Dutch-English
94 pages • 8 1/2 x 11 • $11.95pb • 0-7818-0888-X • (175)

Hippocrene Children's Illustrated French Dictionary
English-French/French-English
94 pages • 8 1/2 x 11 • $11.95pb • 0-7818-0847-2 • (663)

Hippocrene Children's Illustrated German Dictionary
English-German/German-English
94 pages • 8 1/2 x 11 • $11.95pb • 0-7818-0986-X • (570)

Hippocrene Children's Illustrated Irish Dictionary
English-Irish/Irish-English
94 pages • 8 1/2 x 11 • $14.95hc • 0-7818-0713-1 • (798)

Hippocrene Children's Illustrated Italian Dictionary
English-Italian/Italian-English
94 pages • 8 1/2 x 11 • $14.95hc • 0-7818-0771-9 • (355)

Hippocrene Children's Illustrated Norwegian Dictionary
English-Norwegian/Norwegian-English
94 pages • 8 1/2 x 11 • $11.95pb • 0-7818-0887-1 • (165)

Hippocrene Children's Illustrated Polish Dictionary
English-Polish/Polish-English
94 pages • 8 1/2 x 11 • $11.95pbi0-7818-0890-1 • (342)

Hippocrene Children's Illustrated Portuguese Dictionary
English-Portuguese/Portuguese-English
94 pages • 8 1/2 x 11 • $11.95pb • 0-7818-0866-3 • (140)

Hippocrene Children's Illustrated Russian Dictionary
English-Russian/Russian-English
94 pages • 8 1/2 x 11 • $11.95pb • 0-7818-0892-8 • (216)

Hippocrene Children's Illustrated Scottish Gaelic Dictionary
English-Scottish Gaelic/Scottish Gaelic-English
94 pages • 8 1/2 x 11 • $14.95hc • 0-7818-0721-2 • (224)

Hippocrene Children's Illustrated Spanish Dictionary
English-Spanish/Spanish-English
94 pages ó 8 1/2 x 11 ó $11.95pb ó 0-7818-0899-8 • (181)

Hippocrene Children's Illustrated Swedish Dictionary
English-Swedish/Swedish-English
94 pages • 8 1/2 x 11 • $11.95pb • 0-7818-0850-2 • (665)

THE HIPPOCRENE LIBRARY OF WORLD FOLKLORE

Folk Tales from Chile
Brenda Hughes
121 pages • 5 1/2 x 8 1/4 • 15 illustrations • 0-7818-0712-3 • $12.50hc • (785)

Folk Tales from Simla
Alice Elizabeth Dracott
225 pages • 5 3/4 x 8 1/2 • 8 illustrations • 0-7818-0704-2 • $14.95hc • (794)

Swedish Fairy Tales
Baron G. Durklou
190 pages • 5 1/2 x 8 1/4 • 21 illustrations • 0-7818-0717-4 • $12.50hc • (787)

Tales of Languedoc: From the South of France
Samuel Jacques Brun
248 pages • 5 1/2 x 8 1/4 • 33 illustrations • 0-7818-0715-8 • $14.95hc • (793)

Prices subject to change without prior notice. To order **Hippocrene Books**, contact your local bookstore, call (718) 454-2366, visit www.hippocrenebooks.com, or write to: Hippocrene Books, 171 Madison Avenue, New York, NY 10016. Please enclose check or money order adding $5.00 shipping (UPS) for the first book and $.50 for each additional title.